Illustrations © Barbara Layne
Author: Cheryl Simon
Editor: Matthew Koumis
Graphic Design: Rachael Dadd & MK
Reprographics: Ermanno Beverari
Printed in Italy by Grafiche AZ

© Telos Art Publishing 2003

Telos Art Publishing
PO Box 125, Winchester
SO23 7UJ England
t: +44 (0) 1962 864546
f: +44 (0) 1962 864727
e: editorial@telos.net
e: sales@telos.net
w: www.arttextiles.com

ISBN 1 902015 75 4 (softback)

A CIP catalogue record for this book is
available from The British Library

Artist's Acknowledgments
In the past ten years of making art,
the most significant aspect of my practice
has been the dynamic of creation in which
community is formed. Each project has
been accomplished through the
collaborative efforts of friends,
professionals and volunteers who have
committed their time, energy, and
inventive efforts to the realization of the
projects. I am touched by their generosity
and vision and at how these engagements
have enriched my practice and my life.
My thanks to all contributors, collaborators
and participants.

I am grateful to Jake Moore who
sharpened the proverbial pencils that
ensured the completion of this
publication, which has provided an
opportunity for self-reflection and to
exchange ideas with its most generous
writers. I am honored to have Sarah
Quinton's thoughtful introduction and
Cheryl Simon's provocative essay.
Her unique vision and attentive
scholarship provide an unexpected
context in which to consider the work and
define new layers of meaning. I consider
this a gift most extraordinary.

Notes
All dimensions are shown in metric and
imperial, height x width x depth.

Photo Credits
Paul Litherland, Janet Bezzant

Illustration on front cover,
boundary problems
1992
rubber, sawdust, wax
installation
Galerie La Centrale, Montréal

page 1 and 48:
Untitled Study
2002
digital photo of textile objects from the
McCord Museum of Canadian History

About the Author
Cheryl Simon is a Montréal-based artist,
academic and curator who teaches Art
Theory in the MFA program at Concordia
University, and Cinema & Communications
at Dawson College.

This publication was supported in part by
Hexagram: The Institute of Research and
Creation in Media Arts and Technologies
and Concordia University's Scholarly
Development Funds.

portfolio collection
Barbara Layne

TELOS

C O N T E N T S

Hania's Room
(installation detail)
2000
Ukrainian blouse, pool cue

F O R E W O R D BY SARAH QUINTON

Barbara Layne knows textiles. She does this through making them, by traveling and collecting them, by looking at them and talking about them. Who makes textiles and what for? Who uses them? Where can they be found? Who do they belong to? Layne understands the broad possibilities that are conveyed through hand-made and industrially produced textiles, including the social, cultural and intellectual places that textiles hold today. She has contributed to the larger subject of contemporary art and research through the lens of many different modes and materials that, significantly, include cyberspatial encounters that are enlivened through her international network of collaborators. Layne has expanded the limits of accessibility, wherein she (re)distributes textiles via the Internet in a deliberate – yet unpredictable – program of exchange. She circulates digitized information about textile artifacts (both text and image) and creates surprisingly new contexts for them. Her creative project might best be described as a mechanism for the creation of 'democratic wonder' – conversant, challenging and amusing.

This publication outlines work from her 1993 site-specific installation, *Destinations*, to her recent collaborative work, *Inventory of Labour*. *Destinations* was mounted at the Textile Museum of Canada. It was an early exhibition in the history of the Museum's contemporary programming, and one of the first that engaged an exhibiting artist directly with the museum's holdings, which at that time numbered approximately 8000 artifacts. Layne sculpted life-sized beeswax facsimiles of over two dozen tools and textiles such as scissors, shoes, garments and beadwork, which she selected arbitrarily and intuitively to tell a story of intercultural displacement of textile artifacts. With *Inventory of Labour*, she accounts for textile production in the form of a poetic visual analysis of arcane, specialized tools of textile production that she identified during thorough research in the vaults of Montréal's McCord Museum of Canadian History. A revealing aspect of Layne's *Inventory of Labour* is the text she created with Australian scholar and theorist Sue Rowley: "...a digitized field of tools spanning generations of textile hand production. Now heirlooms and museum collections, the tools represent an ambivalent lineage for contemporary practitioners. Leisure and labour, home and factory, the history is etched with the fatigue of gestures and an infinity of desire."

Barbara Layne examines labor and collaboration, the individual and her relationship to the cultural significance of museum collections and the textile-related artifacts in their holdings. These enormous collections are, in the artist's words, "...both attractive and obscene." At times her investigations materialize physically in the gallery context, often through the skilled hands of her collaborators, and at others they are transmitted as virtual information that can be accessed solely through the World Wide Web. She creates new stories and folds them into the lives of the textiles in question. This process closes the gap between the virtual and the physical at the same time as it ensures the regeneration of narratives that will broaden the provenance of the archive.

Barbara Layne has created a broad range of artistic projects over the last ten years. In this publication we see the complexities and passions of her commitment to the study of textiles. Montréal writer Cheryl Simon's text provides a thoughtful blend of analysis and critical response that contextualizes the artist's work in terms of society, culture, museology and artistry. The provision of answers is not Layne's sphere of influence – her ideas are formed and released as she folds and unfolds her cloth: cloth shapes her knowledge and, through her, it assumes new intelligence that vacillates between the intimate and the remote, the mundane and the ethereal.

Sarah Quinton
Contemporary Curator,
Textile Museum of Canada, Toronto

F U T U R E   D I R E C T I O N S

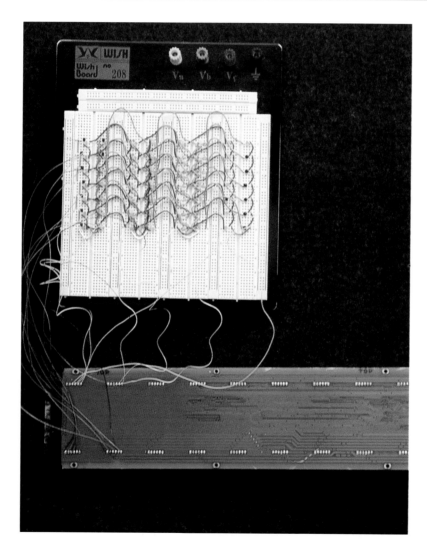

left:

Work in Progress
2002
circuit test

right:
Work in Progress
2002 – ongoing
drawing: color pencil on paper,
10 x 8in (26 x 20.8cm)
sketch of circuitry by Diane Morin

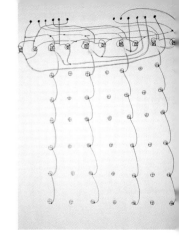

Barbara Layne is a founding member of Hexagram: The Institute for Research and Creation in Media Arts and Technologies, launched in 2001 (www.hexagram.org). Hexagram consists of 60 researchers from 3 universities in Montréal. Interactive Textiles and Wearable Computers is one of 8 axes of research and includes members Ingrid Bachmann, Charles Halary and Joanna Berzowska.

Barbara Layne and her research team (Diane Morin and Jake Moore) are investigating ways of animating fabrics through the introduction of light-emitting diodes, fiber optics and other electronic devices.

The incorporation of sensors and other triggers creates interactive possibilities to examine the fluidity of cultural and physical boundaries. This program of research will embrace an artistic approach to the development of new fabric structures and unique ways of embedding information in cloth. The work will be located in a Fine Arts practice, with the potential for unorthodox applications in industry.

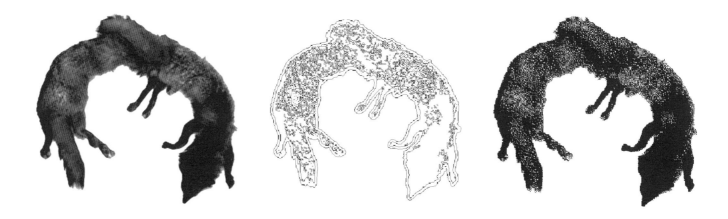

Electronic Textiles: Hacking the Museum
1996
digital image in process

THE PROJECTS

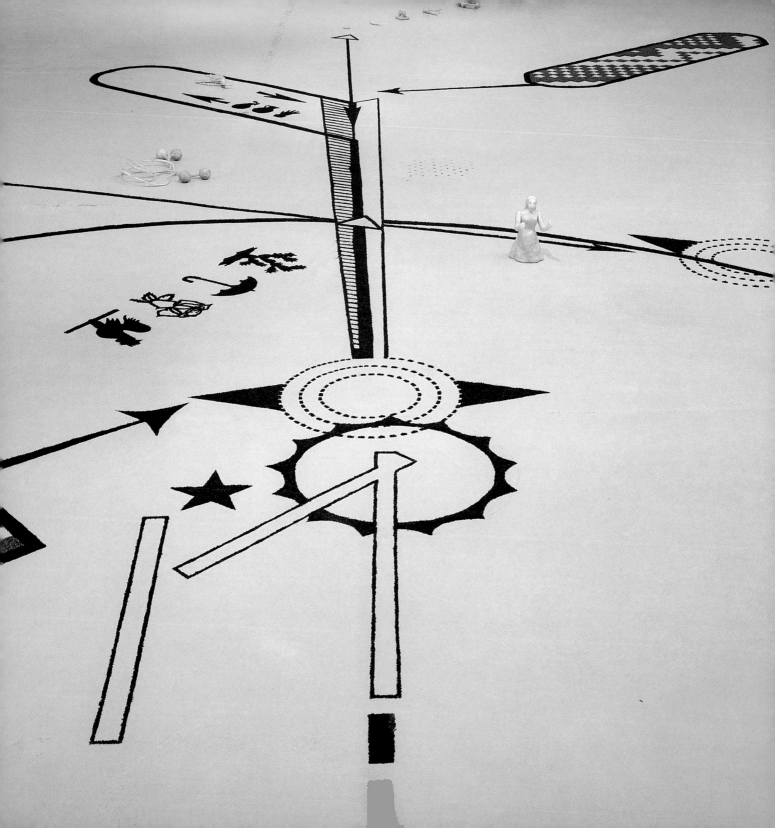

*'Boundary Problems' was installed in 1992 at Galerie
La Centrale in Montréal. Loose rubber bits and dyed
sawdust were arranged to create a floor drawing of Dorval's
International Airport. The runways were inlaid with textile
patterns and technical instructions for weaving and
needlework. Wax replicas of textile objects from the
artists' collection are laid into the diagram on the floor.*

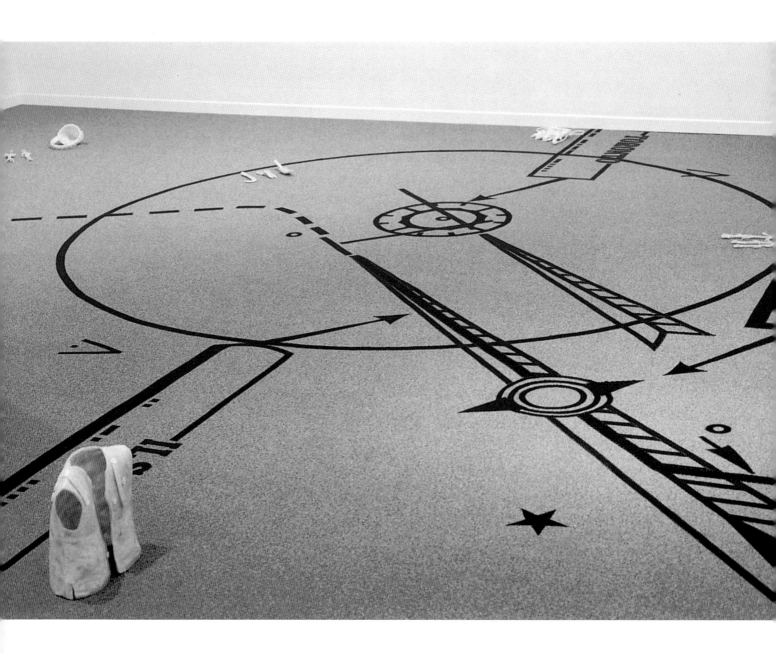

D E S T I N A T I O N S

'Destinations' was installed in 1993 at the Museum for Textiles in Toronto. Black fabric strips form a map of Pearson Airport runways sewn into the industrial carpet. Volunteers from Concordia University, the Ontario College of Art and Sheridan College used curved needles to stitch the fabric to the carpet. Wax replicas of items from the Museum's collection are placed on the floor. The original objects, representing a variety of cultures and geographic locations, were presented in an adjoining space.

POWER

POSITION

TIME
MARK

GAIN

DIRECT-WRITE RECORDER
MODEL VR-1
SERIAL NO. 153

KINEMETRICS

CHINA LAKE

'Fault Lines: Measurement, Distance and Place' was made in collaboration with Ingrid Bachmann in 1995. This telematic weaving project linked galleries La Centrale in Montréal and Side Street Projects in Santa Monica, California. Seismic data was transmitted from geologic labs in Canada and California to the gallery in the alternate country. The data was downloaded into a weaving software program and woven on a computer-assisted handloom. Various weavers operated the loom daily, creating a record of the day's seismic activity. The weave program was an adapted version of ProWeave by Dini Cameron (Cameron Fibre Arts) and an intermediary software program was written by Gordie Ishizuka. More than 80 weavers, programmers, seismologists and others participated in this project.

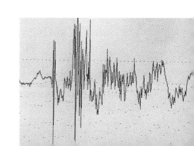

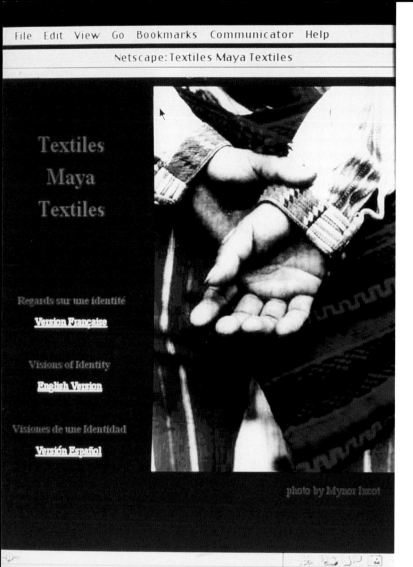

Textiles
Maya
Textiles

Regards sur une identité
Version Française

Visions of Identity
English Version

Visiones de una Identidad
Versión Español

photo by Mynor Ixcot

*'Maya Textiles: Visions of Identity,'
a collaborative curatorial project with
Karen Michelsen, was exhibited at
the Marsil Museum, Québec in 1997.
Textiles from Layne's collection were
displayed in conjunction with selected
texts and images. The images were
culled from a variety of sources,
including a fashion magazine, tourist
postcard and a variety of photographs.
Within each of the large black and
white photos, a single textile was
highlighted with a silk-screened
transparent color. A corresponding
cloth from the collection was
displayed alongside the image and
accompanied by a quote addressing
a particular social situation. These
'visual essays' brought together
disparate fragments, addressing
the production and usage of textiles
within the social context of Guatemala
amidst 30 years of Civil War.*

MAYA TEXTILES

http://alcor.concordia.ca/~textiles

VISIONS OF IDENTITY

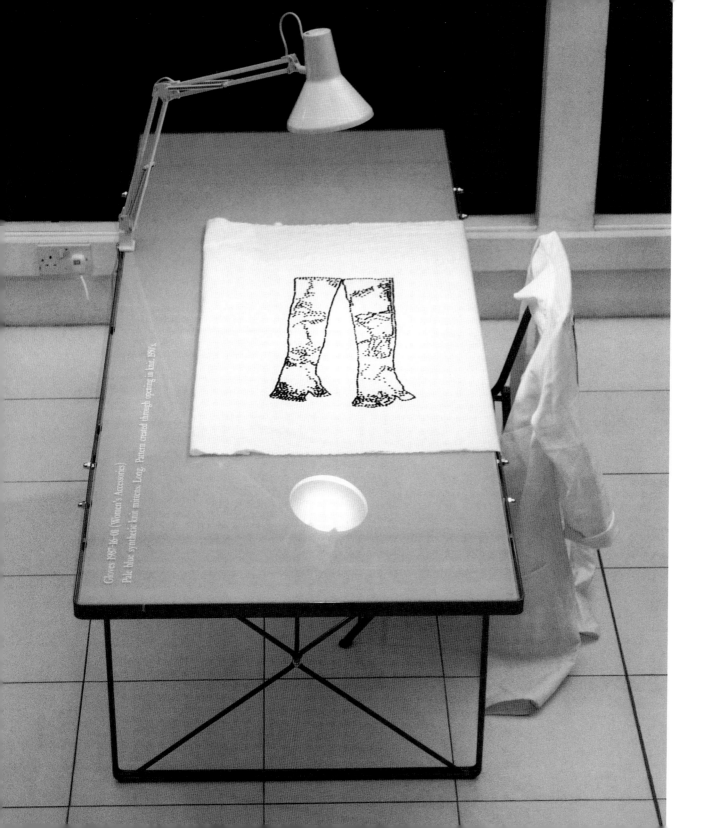

Gloves 1985-46-08 (Women's Accessories)
Pale blue, synthetic knit mittens. Long. Pattern created through opening in knit. 1980s.

'Electronic Textiles: Hacking the Museum' was presented in The Glass Box Gallery in Salford, England during the European Textile Conference in 1996. Images of textile objects from the Marsil Museum, Québec, were digitally photographed, manipulated in Photoshop and transmitted through the Internet to The Glassbox Gallery in Salford. Ten images were downloaded daily for five days. These diagrams were transferred to fabric and several were stitched by an embroidery crew working in the gallery/laboratory. Janet Bezzant facilitated the project and Karen Borland coordinated the participants in Salford.

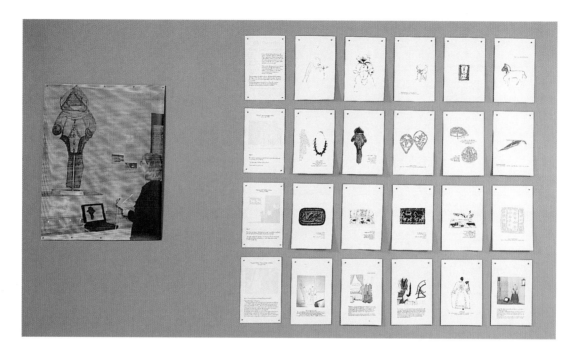

'Drawing Threads' was created for the exhibition 'webs://textiles and new technology' curated by Emily DuBois. Dozens of drawings of textile objects were made in the exhibition galleries at the McCord Museum of Canadian History during the period of January 7 to February 10, 1998. Created with a digital tablet, the images were transmitted weekly through the Internet to the Art Gallery at the University of California in Davis. Technical assistant Lisette de Berry downloaded the drawings and mounted them on the wall for the duration of the exhibition.

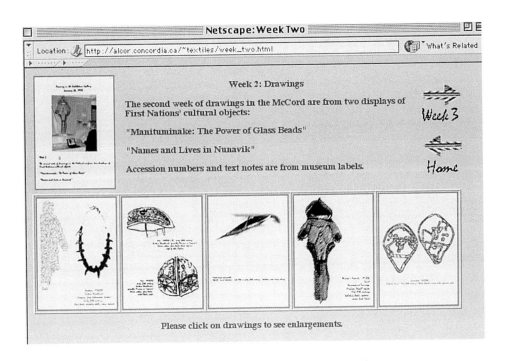

Week 2: Drawings

The second week of drawings in the McCord are from two displays of First Nations' cultural objects:

"Manituminake: The Power of Glass Beads"

"Names and Lives in Nunavik"

Accession numbers and text notes are from museum labels.

Please click on drawings to see enlargements.

http://alcor.concordia.ca/~textiles/drawing.html

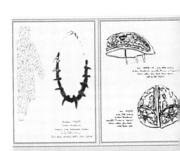

'Hania's Room' (1999), was presented in the exhibition '48 Hours 48 Rooms' in Montréal. Curated by Ingrid Bachmann, each artist was invited to transform a room in a vacant boarding house. 'Hania's Room' included a faux fireplace with bowling pins, an embroidered Ukrainian blouse hung from a pool cue, photographs mounted in backlit windows, a simmering pot of borscht on the stove, and a wall text which read:

> "Hania's family left the Ukraine upon hearing there was an infinite supply of firewood in Canada. They settled in Tomahawk, Alberta. She changed her name. She married an American and moved to the high plains desert of eastern Oregon. Bob built a bowling alley. Anne ran the snack bar.
>
> Each night they burned an endless supply of worn-out bowling pins in the fireplace."

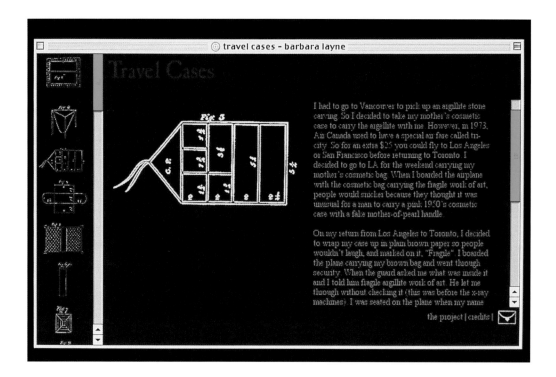

'Travel Cases' was developed for the online project, Science Fair:
Feminist Interventions in Cyberspace, curated by Lorraine Oades in
2002. This web site combines a collection of images from the past
with contemporary urban stories. Diagrams from the Workwoman's
Guide, published at the end of the 19th century, provide an entrance
to the work. These images are blueprints for the construction of hand-
sewn objects used to protect and transport everyday items: a shoebag,
a book cover, a sewing box, etc. Each object links to a contemporary
story told by participants at the Banff Centre for the Arts in the
summer of 1993. The site was designed by Brazen with Adriana
Miranda leading the creative team.

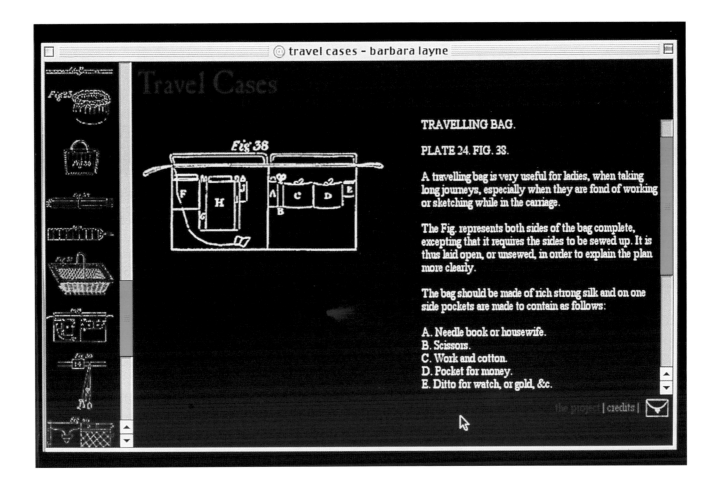

@ travel cases - barbara layne

Travel Cases

Fig 38

TRAVELLING BAG.

PLATE 24. FIG. 38.

A travelling bag is very useful for ladies, when taking long journeys, especially when they are fond of working or sketching while in the carriage.

The Fig. represents both sides of the bag complete, excepting that it requires the sides to be sewed up. It is thus laid open, or unsewed, in order to explain the plan more clearly.

The bag should be made of rich strong silk and on one side pockets are made to contain as follows:

A. Needle book or housewife.
B. Scissors.
C. Work and cotton.
D. Pocket for money.
E. Ditto for watch, or gold, &c.

the project | credits |

http://www.studioxx.org/sciencefair

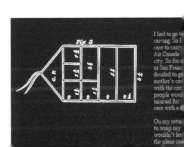

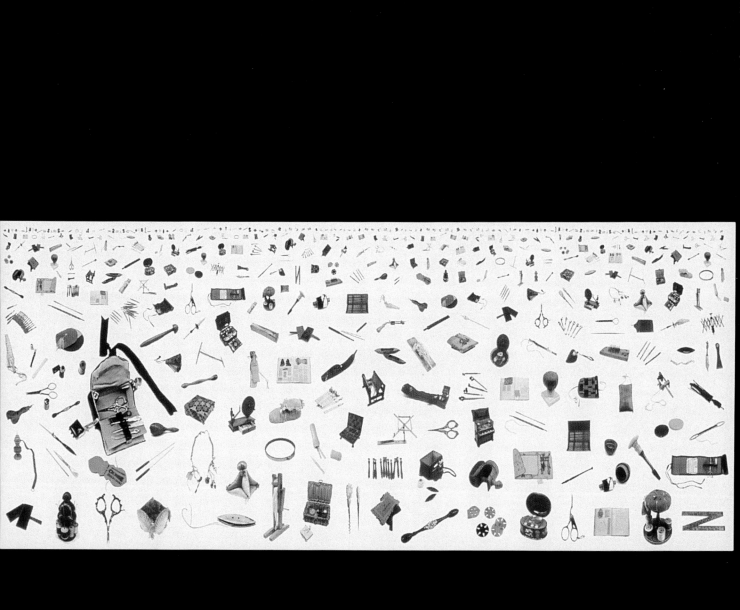

'Inventory of Labour' consists of artists' pages made in collaboration with Sue Rowley for the anthology, Objects of Labor (edited by Joan Livingstone and John Ploof, Chicago, SAIC Press, 2003/4). Textile tools from the McCord Museum for Canadian History were digitally photographed and manipulated into a landscape. An accompanying text refers to "a digitized field of tools spanning generations of textile hand production. Now heirlooms and museum collections, the tools represent an ambivalent lineage for contemporary practitioners. Leisure and labor, home and factory, the history is etched with the fatigue of gestures and an infinity of desire."

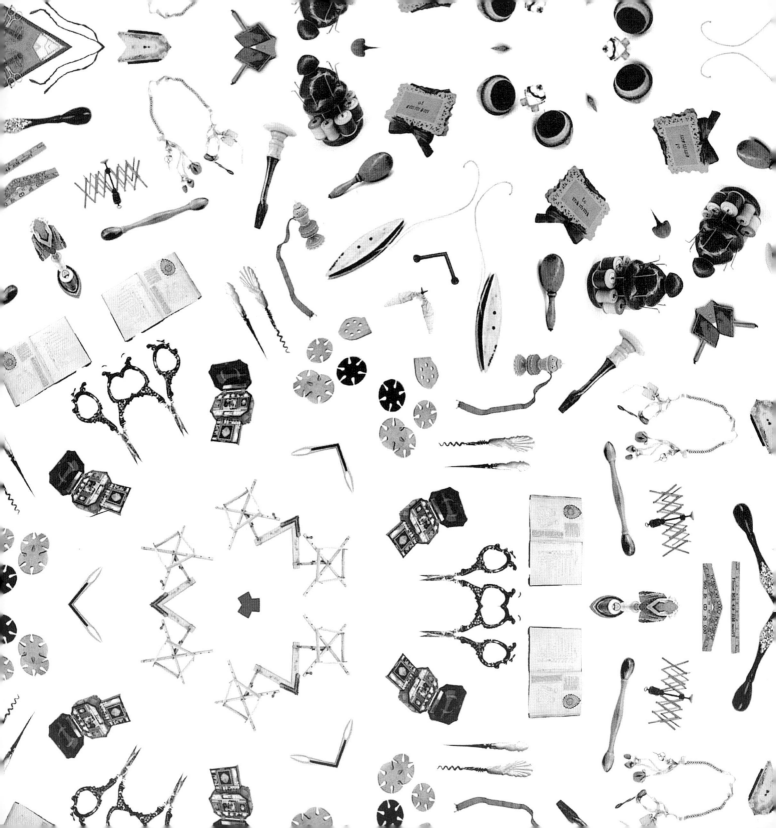

MOVING THINGS:

THE COLLECTIONS OF BARBARA LAYNE

BY CHERYL SIMON

Boundary Problems
(installation detail, see also pages 34-5)
1992
black rubber, dyed sawdust, beeswax

Introduction

Barbara Layne makes art about artifacts. Concerned with the powerful and dynamic relationship we have with things – collectively and individually – the artist's practice seeks new means of accounting for and representing the products of a wide range of cultural endeavors.

An art interpretation, of translation and transformation, replication and revitalization, Layne has sculpted facsimiles of handcrafted textiles, tools and statuary out of aromatic beeswax, and carved diagrams of airport runways and textile pattern instructions into dark, deep mats of rubber granules laid out on gallery floors. With collaborators she has woven graphic representations of seismic activity occurring across the North American continent into elegant tapestries, and orchestrated the embroidery reconstitution of Canadian textile artifacts from scanned imagery transmitted electronically overseas. Recently, the artist has employed 19th century sewing guidebooks to inspire a rich collection of stories and anecdotes memorializing individual encounters with domestic ephemera, and threaded looms with vibrant electronic circuitry to illustrate the historical memory of cloth.

Notwithstanding the extraordinary aesthetic resonance of the things Layne makes, the original material qualities and specific use functions of the artifacts that she copies are always secondary in importance to the particular meanings and values that have been attributed to them, meanings and values that are seen to change over time and in different circumstances. As objects/textiles change hands – as they are produced, used, traded, collected, displayed or represented – so is their significance transformed, and it is the changeability of things and their altered meanings rather than their essence that her work seeks to highlight. Thus Layne's presentations are always, necessarily, representations, interpretations of objects caught in transition.

Part I: The Artist, The Collection & The Museum

Layne's practice might best be defined as a form of experimental museology, the principle interests of which lie with the social life of objects in general, and textile objects in particular. Over the last several years the artist has, in fact, produced her works in association with various museums, occupying the relatively new role of artist/curator. In this regard, Layne's practice reflects a shift in the manner in which artists have come to engage the museum as a subject in their work. More collaborative than combative, thus significantly different from the relationship held by historical and recent avant-gardes with the museum, the work is nonetheless informed by the various expressions of institutional critique that preceded it – in conceptual art and minimalism, in particular the site-works and performance art practices of the 1970s and 1980s, as well as in early and recent feminist criticism. Nevertheless, the museum itself no longer represents the primary object of censure for contemporary artists. Rather, as Miwon Kwon has observed, it has come to function as a staging ground for "a critique of culture that is inclusive of non-art spaces, non-art institutions, non-art issues (blurring the division between art and non-art, in fact)." In turn, Layne's work might be said to elaborate the museological in culture more generally, taking the museum as both symptom and metaphor of contemporary life.

Early works in Layne's project considered the journey of objects through the world quite literally, exploring the fate of the cultural artifact in the face of geo-physical displacement in the act of collection and representation, in other words. *Boundary Problems*, made in 1992, shortly after the artist immigrated to Canada from the US, and *Destinations*, produced a year later, installed life-size, hand-sculpted beeswax replicas of a wide range of objects on room-size 'Jeppeson' maps of airport runways, the touchdown points and compass markings intersecting with instructions for weaving patterns and other handicraft.

In *Boundary Problems* the objects

replicated and dispersed along the runways were things the artist had accumulated over a lifetime of travel, mementoes from other times and places, object surrogates for the experiences that had shaped Layne's life before immigration. The sculptural elements of *Destinations* copied objects belonging to the Museum for Textiles in Toronto where they stood in for times and places given to define cultural collectives as a whole. Domestic and foreign, familiar and exotic, toys and tools, trinkets and cloth: but for the differences in specific sizes and shapes, the beeswax standardized the physical attributes of the individual objects. If the historical and geo-physical particularity of individual cultural artifacts brought together in the collection necessarily gives way to the historical interests and attitudes of the collector, the orientation and impact of this perspective cannot be predicted in advance. Hence, the objects Layne cast in these installations were scattered across several different directional points on the runway maps, laid open to a range of interpretations and re-presentations encouraged by the corresponding variety of points-of-view attending their reception.

The collection is not constructed by its elements; rather it comes to exist by means of its principles of organization. If that principle is bounded at the onset of the collection, the collection will be finite, or at least potentially finite. If that principle tends toward infinity or the series itself, the collection will be open-ended.
Susan Stewart

A tiny box of falling stars promises an infinity of destinations. Navigating through the hypertext and the hype, my right hand points to unimaginable sites. As I race through this new world, the pattern of the seat cushion becomes embossed on the back of my motionless legs. My body stiffens like a forgotten textile that longs to be opened and refolded along new lines.

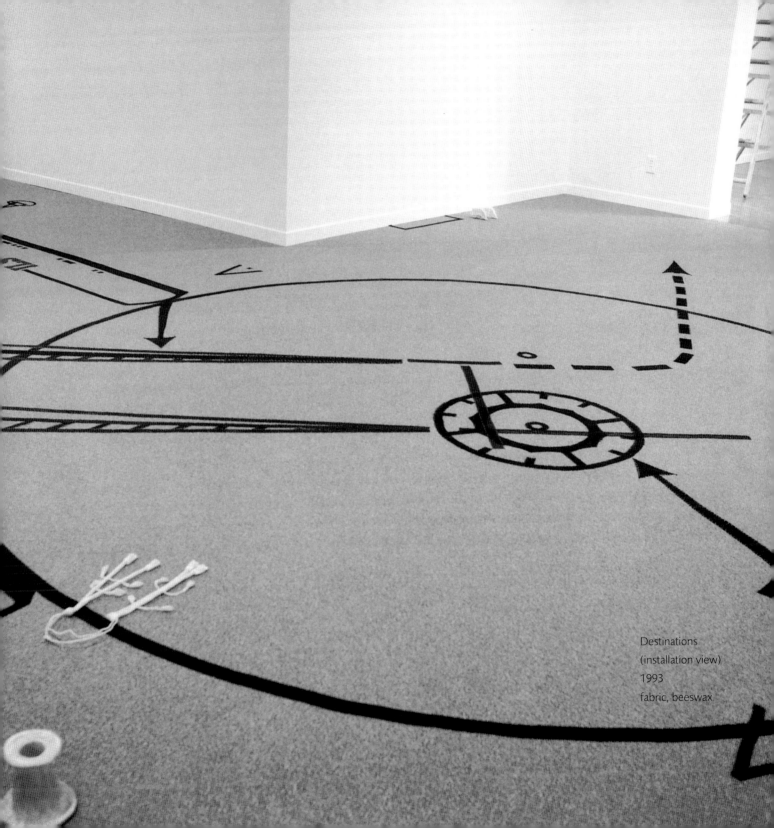

Destinations
(installation view)
1993
fabric, beeswax

Moving from the terminal to the mound of cloth, I begin to sort, smooth, count, fold and stack. Time slows down. My left hand pauses on the image of a double-headed bird in the corner of a well-worn cloth. I am once again connected to a place where all other places exist.
Barbara Layne

A metaphor for the spatial conditions of the collection in the earlier works, distance was engaged as a literal and strategic component of *Fault Lines: Measurement, Distance and Place*, a collaborative work made with Ingrid Bachmann in 1995.

Involving the electronic exchange of data registering seismic activity in Montréal and Santa Monica, and its transformation into fabrics through weavers operating computer-generated looms at each site, the project offered a compelling exploration of the material, cultural and social components of production.

Sensitive to every footfall, every loom movement, and, of course, the constant shifts in the earth's crust, as the objects produced in *Fault Lines* measured the expression of space across time, they revealed the relationship between far-ranging cultural communities to be interactive, dynamic and ever-changing, subject to an infinite number of factors and circumstances.

By extension, so too was the relationship between cultural producers and the things they produce defined. *Fault Lines* was a highly ambivalent work. At the same time it was a work of art and an ongoing social activity, a hand-made artifact and technologically generated representation, the expression of human actions and natural phenomena. Because of this the work resisted easy classification. Impossible to categorize, it was even more hopeless to contain.

*...**Fault Lines** worked so well because it was an actual example of something that works, a living lesson in how to make something connect with itself and reality (or rather how not to disconnect in the first place). What counts is the fact that something with its own dynamic is produced, something new, something which connects with reality simply by virtue of the extent to which it sets up loops with itself, feeding back into the processes which compose it, and extending itself far beyond the gallery, the individual artists, the critics, and even its own end products.*
Sadie Plant

Part II:
Performing The Museum

Museums will continue to be highly
problematic and we will still be
magnetically drawn to them. Who
is not transfixed by the sight of the
temple of Dendur, the 15th- century
BC temple and gate from Egypt,
relocated stone by stone to
the Metropolitan Museum of Art?
And I can still recall the excitement
of holding down the painfully stiff
button on the glass case at the
Brooklyn Museum of Art that provides
the dim lighting for viewing the barely
visible and utterly miraculous
needle-knitted Paracas Textile.
Barbara Layne

If Layne admits ambivalence with
regard to the cultural productions of
the museum, her insistence on the
hand fashioning of her reproductions
reveals some hesitation regarding the
value of technological representation
as well. Layne would seem to share
Walter Benjamin's concerns for the
loss of immediate, material experience
in an era of mass, mechanical
reproducibility. Yet the artist also uses
technology as a means to permit
greater cultural participation and
exchange, again like Benjamin,
expressing optimism regarding the
democratic possibilities of new
technologies. In fact, such
ambivalence recognizes the trade-off
inherent in art conceived as
representation: what is lost to the
object's cult value – its historical
locatedness – is gained in the
object's increased exhibitionibility.
To acknowledge the allegorical
functioning of both art and historical
artifacts is to recognize that artifacts
in museums and objects in
reproduction behave first and
foremost as expressions of historical
processes – of loss, but also
of transformation in both social
transactions and cultural life.

Layne's various 'telematic' projects
have looked to the Internet as a means
to expand the interpretive and
participatory role of the museum.
However, the electronic exchange
of information is only one step in a
longer, more involved process of
interpretation and representation,
of the artifacts themselves and, more
significantly, of the practices of
collecting and classification – hence
the artist refers to her practice as
'performing the museum'.

In *Electronic Textiles: Hacking the*
Museum (1996), the artist
photographed a selection of textile
objects from the holdings of the Marsil
Museum in Québec, altered and
transmitted these images, along with
their card catalog descriptions, to The
Glass Box Gallery at the University of
Salford in England, where a team
of 'gallery technicians' reconstituted
the received imagery through hand
embroidery. Dematerialized
technologically, altered and
rematerialized by human beings, at
each interface the shape and substance
of the object was transformed.
Information was gained and lost
through the photography, the file
translation and data transmission,
showing up as more or less subtle
distortions in the surface characteristics
of the objects depicted in the
transmitted imagery.

Similarly, details were added to and ignored at the point of reconstitution: if nothing else, the individual style of each of the technicians' stitching would interpret the objects differently. This is not to say that the resulting objects were inadequate representations of the fur stoles and evening clothes, top hats and nurses' caps initially sent along this journey; on the contrary. This is to say that the translated objects expressed the social and cultural experience of the objects in their present situation, still signifiers for the times and places described by the museum's card catalog, but now also expressions of the desires and fantasies, historical experience and values of the exhibition's participants.

In *Drawing Threads* Layne took another approach to 'performing the museum', this time focusing on the object's interpretation at the point of reception. Over a four-week period in the winter of 1998 Layne took up residence in the McCord Museum of Canadian History and, armed with a laptop computer and a graphics tablet, produced a sketch survey of the exhibitions presented by the museum. At weekly intervals the drawings were sent by the Internet to the University of California-Davis Design Gallery, printed and mounted on the walls. Week one presented the artist's preliminary drawings, while weeks two through four alternated sketches of exhibitions of First Nations cultural artifacts with representations of exhibitions of French and Anglo-Canadian folk art and costumes.

Significantly, *Drawing Threads* made no attempt to compensate for the dematerialization of the artifacts it represented by reconstituting them. This was an exhibition which took as its subject a group of exhibitions, and the drawings were careful to recognize this by including the accession numbers and text notes from the museum's labels on the same sketch pages. Instead, it could be said that *Drawing Threads* attempted to translate the experience of the museum itself, to capture the thrill and fascination of discovering the familiar in foreign things. Layne drew what drew her to the objects in the exhibitions in the first place: the qualities of the materials used to manufacture the artifacts, the ingenuity of design and impressive craft employed in their making, but also the compelling discontinuity and non-synchronicity of the museum's objects, cultures, places and times.

The problems of historical interpretation posed by traditional modes of classification and interpretation are more pointed in exhibitions of contemporary cultural artifacts. This problem is even more basic for exhibitions of cultural artifacts from foreign cultures, and especially cultures whose traditions and practices are more typically subject to historical subjugation in ethnographic exhibitions. Not only is it difficult to appreciate the historical significance of objects still in circulation, but also the act of representation takes things out of circulation prematurely, fixing objects (and the cultures they represent) in the time of past rather than present circumstances.

Every description or interpretation that conceives itself as 'bringing culture into writing,' moving from oral-discursive experience... to a written version of that experience... is enacting the structure of salvage. To the extent that the ethnographic process is seen as inscription, the representation will continue to enact a potent, and questionable, allegorical structure.
James Clifford

When Layne adopted the persona of the curator for *Maya Textiles: Visions*

of Identity (1997), an exhibition and Web Project produced in collaboration with Karen Michelsen for the Marsil Museum, she confronted these problems head-on. Michelsen suggested a strategy similar in kind to that Layne herself had used in previous work: to approach the exhibition in allegorical terms. In addition to the textiles themselves the exhibition included a range of other representations: textual elements from various literature on Guatemala, its past and present circumstances, history and people as well as photographs of the types of garments on display, as they appear in contemporary life, and in a range of other, often more mythical visual descriptions. Offering a range of perspectives on the textiles, and the culture within which they circulate, these doubled-up representations effectively situated the artifacts within an ongoing and active economy of representation.

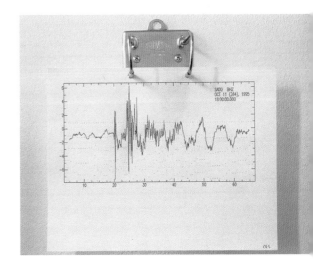

Fault Lines: Measurement, Distance and Place
(installation detail)
1995
printout of seismic event

Part III: History From Things

Whereas iconography, the analysis of subject matter, serves an art historian in discerning and tracking linkages of objects across time and space, the analysis of style facilitates the identification of difference in elements that are specific to a place, a time, a maker...

Style is most informative about underlying beliefs when their expression is least self-conscious, and a society is less self-conscious in what it makes, especially such utilitarian objects as houses, furniture and pots, than in what it says or does, which is necessarily conscious and intentional.
Jules David Prown

Long concerned with the symbolic forms and function of objects and the role that they play in the production of individual and collective histories, Layne has recently turned her attention more to the historical transformations expressed in and by things themselves.

Practicing her fieldwork in the spaces of everyday life, the artist has begun to look more closely at things both domestic and familiar. *Hania's Room* (1999) told the story of her mother's migration from the Ukraine to the US, via Canada, here refracted through a selection of objects given to characterize Hania's life. This was a story about dreams and actualities, anticipated paths and their inevitable diversions. Hence, the object surrogates for Hania's experience were also marked by modification. Signaled by the hybridization and transformation of Layne's mother's apparel, the correspondence between changing cultural identifications and class situations was epitomized in a lushly embroidered Ukrainian blouse transformed into a waitress uniform-cum-bowling shirt by the addition of a pair of names stitched onto the lapels. Most mournfully, bowling pins slated for firewood signaled the accommodation of the immigrating family's dreams to the economic realities of their new homeland.

Hania's Room was also a story about social and cultural transformation in contemporary life. Produced for an exhibition marking the conversion of a low-income rooming house into a luxury condominium complex, the installation not only considered the effects of dislocation expressed in the loss of language and culture but even more crucially as they are experienced through the body, a point underscored by Layne's performance in the exhibition. Triggering intimate associations with the lost comforts of home, Layne served fragrant beet borscht to visitors to *Hania's Room*.

Biographies of things can make salient what might otherwise remain obscure. For example, in situations of culture contact, they can show what anthropologists have so often stressed: that what is significant about the adoption of alien objects – as of alien ideas – is not the fact that they are adopted, but the way they are culturally redefined and put to use.
Igor Kopytoff

Travel Cases (2002), an Internet project recently developed by Layne, offers an opportunity to observe cultural differences and historical shifts through encounters with a range of hand-sewn objects and the stories they inspired. The web site links instructions for the making of a variety of 19th - century travel cases with a collection of anecdotes told to Layne by colleagues and friends. Here the descriptions for richly perfumed handkerchief sleeves, family nightgown bags and seaman's cases with pockets for both sewing materials and fishhooks, "useful for all classes and schoolboys," call to mind a stable, well ordered world of clear foresight and careful planning. It's a world where every object, like its owners, had a clearly defined place within it and every journey away from home promised a return.

In contrast, the stories inspired by the cases describe a very different place, less orderly and less certain: not a world of perfectly laid plans for perfectly stitched pockets, but one filled with recycled things and emotional stories of families and friends. The seaman's case reminds its respondent of a seaman's trunk that she played house in as a child. And the trunk, in turn, reminds her of its owner, a father she came to know through the things he'd left behind. For another, a 'traveling dressing case' brings to mind a comic misadventure about a man who used his mother's cosmetic case to safeguard a precious object on an airplane trip. The traveling cases – those imagined and those remembered – mark time through difference: the difference between generations and places, between ideas and reality, plans and their actualization.

That history is a process of repetition and transformation – whether in the production or accumulation of anecdotes, ideas or things – is a concept that grounds all of Layne's works. However, *Inventory of Labour* (2003), an artists' page work made in collaboration with Sue Rowley, and *Interactive Textiles* (2002), a program of research involving the production of electronic cloth, make this point directly, looking for the expression of historical change in the processes and products of textile art.

Inventory of Labour presents an array of images of textile tools positioned at equal intervals across a gatefold page. Decreasing in size on the vertical axis, the arrangement suggests that the rows of tools extend beyond the horizon line. All are tools worked by hand, and all are scaled accordingly, each laid out in a regular pattern, the same but different, repeating themselves, although differently each time, making new patterns and arrangements out of old. If the work mimics the actions of the craftwork for which the tools are used, and the gestures of textile labor beat a syncopated rhythm that conveys the ambivalent nature of the work, as Sue Rowley has suggested, they also express the nature of historical movement. History repeats itself: transformation is born of ideas that take hold only if practiced in the repetitive gestures of everyday life.

While textiles are not always the explicit subjects of Layne's work, they invariably inform the way it will be conceived or realized. The artist thinks through textiles. She looks for patterns in cultural practices, builds webs of communities, draws threads between objects and ideas, ideas and people, and weaves media together in ways that are always new and provocative. Mark Newport has noted how Layne's use of textile metaphors in her Internet work has productively cast both technologies in new light: "Her cloth is electronic pulses and bits of data delivered through a net of wires and cables that provides millions of points of contact to communicate its message."

Layne's current program of research may just actualize these metaphors. With *Interactive Textiles* the artist has begun to weave cloth using electronic circuitry. The plan is to animate the fabric creating patterns programmed to metamorphoze into other designs, in this way illuminating the course of historical transformation. As Layne's textile metaphors have mapped technological forms in cyberspace, her electronic textiles production promises a measurement of time in material practice.

Textiles are not the cargo that is transported in our personal baggage but a vehicle in which to become more fully engaged in the experience of being. We can become mesmerized in the folds, hold conversations in the web, and find complications in the texture. They tell the stories of a vintage Dior in a pile of unsorted thrift-store clothing, of being rooted in a wool plaid, flirting along the bouncy hem of a flared skirt, or admiring the brilliant red algodon that is the resilience of the Maya.
Barbara Layne

right:

Boundary Problems
(installation view)
1992
black rubber, dyed sawdust, beeswax

The author would like to thank Fred McSherry and Barbara Layne for reading and commenting on this essay at different stages. And thanks especially to Barbara Layne for the picnic lunches where she introduced me to her many marvelous works.

James Clifford, "On Ethnographic Allegory," in *Writing Culture: The Poetics and Politics of Ethnography*, ed. James Clifford and George E. Marcus (Berkeley: University of California Press, 1986), 113.

Igor Kopytoff, "The Cultural Biography of Things: Commoditization As Process," in *The Social Life of Things: Commodities in Perspective*, ed. Arjun Appardurai (Cambridge: Cambridge University Press, 1989), 67.

Miwon Kwon, "One Place After Another: Notes on Site Specificity," *October 80* (Spring 1997), 85-110, 91.

Barbara Layne, *The Presence of Touch* (Chicago: The School of the Art Institute, 1996), 18.

Barbara Layne, "Migrant Textiles: Burdens, Bundles, Baggage," ed. Janis Jefferies, *Reinventing Textiles, Vol. 2, Gender and Identity* (Winchester, England: Telos Art Publishing, 2001), 87, 89.

Mark Newport, "The Future is Past: Textiles and New Technologies," *Fiberarts* (September/October, 1998), 57.

Sadie Plant, "The Good, the Bad and the Productive," eds. Ine Gevers and Jeanne van Heeswijk, *Beyond Ethics and Aesthetics* (SUN 1997), 356.

Jules David Prown, "The Truth of Material Culture," *History from Things: Essays on Material Culture*, eds Steven Lubar and W. David Kingery (Washington and London: Smithsonian Institution Press, 1993), 5.

Susan Stewart, *On Longing: Narratives of the Miniature, the Gigantic, the Souvenir and the Collection* (Johns Hopkins, 1985) 155.

B I O G R A P H Y

Born

1952   Seattle, Washington. Lives in Canada and Mexico

Education

1976-79   University of Colorado, Boulder, BFA
1980-82   University of Kansas, Lawrence, MFA

Grants and Fellowships

2002   Hexagram: The Institute for Research and Creation in Media Arts and Technologies, Individual Research Grant

Fonds de recherche sur la société et la culture, Regroupement stratégique grant, Team Grant

Canadian Foundation for Innovation, Principal Investigator of Team

2001   Province of Québec, Valorisation Recherche Québec, Team Grant

Development Funds, Ministere de la Metropole (City of Montréal), Team Grant

2000   Daniel Langlois Foundation for Art, Science & Technology Exhibition Fund, Team Grant

1998   The Canada Council for the Arts, Travel Grant

Conseil des arts et des lettres du Québec, B Grant

Social Sciences and Humanities Research Council, Travel Grant

1996   Conseil des arts et des lettres du Québec, Travel Grant

1993   The Banff Centre for the Arts, Luis Muhlstock Fellowship

The Canada Council for the Arts, Project Grant 1995

The Canada Council for the Arts, Computer Integrated Media Grant

Selected Solo Exhibitions and Collaborative Projects

2003	'Inventory of Labour', artists' pages, collaboration with Sue Rowley, 'Objects of Labor,' J. Livingstone, J. Ploof, eds, Chicago: SAIC Press
2002	'Travel Cases', web project for Science Fair, curated by Lorraine Oades for Studio XX
1997	'Maya Textiles: Visions of Identity', collaborative project with Karen Michelsen, Marsil Museum of Textiles, Québec
1996	'Electronic Textiles: Hacking the Museum', The Glass Box Gallery, Salford, England
1995	'Fault Lines: Measurement, Distance and Place', collaborative work with Ingrid Bachmann, connecting Side Street Projects, Santa Monica, CA and Galerie La Centrale, Montréal
	'Fault Lines: Measurement, Distance and Place', collaborative work with Ingrid Bachmann, connecting Side Street Projects, Santa Monica, CA and Galerie La Centrale, Montréal
1992	'Boundary Problems', Galerie La Centrale, Montréal, Québec
1984	'1-5 Phase Lag', Southeastern Center for Contemporary Art, Winston-Salem, North Carolina

Selected Group Exhibitions

2001	'Border Crossings,' White Mountain Academy of the Arts, Elliot Lake, Ontario
1999	'48 Hours 48 Rooms,' Alternative site, Montréal, Québec
	'Textiles/TECHSTYLES,' Saratoga Arts Center, New York
1998	'webs://textiles and new technology,' University of California Art Gallery, Davis, California
1997	'Splice,' Side Street Projects Gallery, Santa Monica, California
	'The Presence of Touch,' Gallery 2, Chicago, Illinois
1992	'Speaking In Tongues,' The InterArt Center, New York, New York
	'Needle Expressions,' Nelson Fine Arts Center, Tempe, Arizona
	'Influences – Innovation,' Torpedo Factory Arts Center, Alexandria, Virginia
1986	'First International Biennale of Paper Art,' Leopold-Hoesch Museum, Düren, Germany
	'Postscriptum/Librifibra/Fiberbooks,' Studio E Gallery, Rome, Italy
1985	'Fibers East/Fibers West,' Fiberworks Center for Textile Arts, Berkeley, California
	'Textile as Sculpture – 12th International Biennial of Tapestry,' Musée Cantonal des Beaux Arts, Lausanne, Switzerland

Selected Writings

2001	'Migrant Textiles: Burdens, Bundles and Baggage,' *Reinventing textiles: tradition and innovation,* edited by Janis Jefferies, Telos Art Publishing, Winchester, England
2000	'Interpolations,' Interviews with 6 artists, e-textiles CD-ROM, Centre for Contemporary Textiles of Montréal
1999	'Electronic Textiles: Hacking the Museum, Creating Textiles: Makers, Methods, Markets,' Textile Society of America
1989	'Extraordinarily Fashionable,' *New Art Examiner*
1986	'American Paper Art,' *First International Biennial of Paper Art Catalogue*, Düren, Germany

Citation/Reviews

2002	*Surface Design Journal*, 'Cyber/Fyber/Text,' by Cheryl Kolak-Dudek
2001	'Re-Verberations Dislocutions: Interim Entries' for a
	Dictionnaire Elémentaire on cultural translation, by Sarat Maharaj
2000	*International Tapestry Journal*, 'The Translation of Textiles in the Electronic Field,'
	by Diana Wood Conroy and Dr. Kurt Brereton, Australia
1998	*Fiberarts*, 'The Future is Past,' by Mark Newport
	'Beyond Ethics and Aesthetics, The Good, the Bad and the Productive,' by Sadie Plant
1997	*Craft Victoria*, 'The Body Image,' by Patrick Snelling, Australia
	Splice, exhibition catalog., Side Street Projects publication
1996	*EXPANDING CIRCLES: Women, Art and Community*,
	'Gatekeepers, Silences, and Freedom,' by Betty Ann Brown
	F Newsmagazine, 'The Presence of Touch,' by Gwendolyn F. Zierdt
	Transmission, 'Turbulent Matter/s,' by Kim Sawchuk, La Centrale publication
	Fiberarts Magazine, 'Electronic Textiles: New Possibilities,' by Margo Mensing
	Parachute Magazine, 'Barbara Layne and Ingrid Bachmann,' by Kim Sawchuk
1991	*Textilkunst Magazine*, 'Barbara Layne: Mixed Messages,' by Jennifer Salahub

Professional

Associate Professor, Department of Studio Arts, Concordia University, Montréal, Québec
International Advisor, 'Side Street' (online journal)
Founding Member, Hexagram,
the Institute for Research and Creation in Media Arts and Technologies